Carving Dolphins and Whales

Dale Power

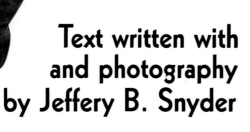

Text written with
and photography
by Jeffery B. Snyder

D1609688

Schiffer Publishing Ltd

77 Lower Valley Road, Atglen, PA 19310

ONTENTS

Copyright © 1994 by
Dale L. Power
Library of Congress Catalog Number: 94-65851

Printed in China
ISBN: 0-88740-620-3

We are interested in hearing from authors
with book ideas on related topics.

Published by Schiffer Publishing Ltd.
77 Lower Valley Road
Atglen, PA 19310
Please write for a free catalog.
This book may be purchased from the publisher.
Please include $2.95 postage.
Try your bookstore first.

INTRODUCTION

Dolphins are popular with everyone, their carefree nature makes them favorites to watch. They love to play and will cavort with anything from feathers to people.

Dolphins and whales are classified as cetaceans, or sea mammals. They are not fish. Dolphins are some of the smallest of the whales, measuring only twelve feet long, while the blue whales are some of the largest at over one hundred feet in length.

Male whales are called bulls, females are termed cows and their young are dubbed calves. (Sound familiar?) Dolphins and Killer Whales are classified in the tooth whale group. The Wright and Blue whales are baleen whales.

Whales and fish swim differently. Fish move their tails from side-to-side while whales move theirs up and down. Unlike fish, dolphins are also tapered at the front and back ends so that water flows easily over the whole body. There are no flat surfaces on their bodies.

Because dolphins and whales spend most of their time under water, little is known about their lives in the wild. Most of our information has been gained by observing them in captivity.

This dolphin is carved out of Basswood, also known as American Linden. Basswood is classified as a hardwood, but it works well for either hand or machine carving. Working with Basswood helps ensure a durable and high quality finished product.

Speaking of carving, I use a bench knife, a set of assorted hand gouges, an Automat Power Chisel, a Detail Master Wood Burning System, a Foredom flexible shaft machine, and an Optima-2 high speed grinder. Both the Foredom and the Optima-2 are fitted with assorted carbide burrs for this project. The paints are acrylic washes.

Whenever you use sharp tools a Kevlar woodcarvers glove is a wise choice to protect your hand from the blade. **However, it is important to remember NEVER to use the glove with rotary power tools. The potential for getting the burr wrapped in the glove, causing serious personal injury, is simply too great.**

It is always wise to protect your lungs with a dust mask or a dust collection system when you use power tools.

Good luck carving your Dolphin.

CARVING THE DOLPHIN

Before carving animals (or any subject for that matter), find as many photos of each animal you wish to carve as possible to make the carving easier and to add authenticity and life to your work. I suggest sporting magazines and children's books on animals as terrific source materials.

Having done my research, the dolphin I have chosen to carve here is a Bottle-nosed Dolphin (a.k.a. Bottle-nosed Porpoise or Gray Porpoise), ranging from 8 to 12 feet (3.7 meters) in length. It is a robust mammal which may have its name prefixed by either "Atlantic" or "Pacific". It feeds on a wide variety of fish, squid, shrimp and crabs. Bottle-nosed Dolphins range from Newfoundland to Venezuela-- including the Gulf of Mexico--in the Atlantic and in the Pacific from Southern California to the tropics.

To transfer the pattern to the wood, carbon paper may be used. We also want to draw the body of the dolphin three times.

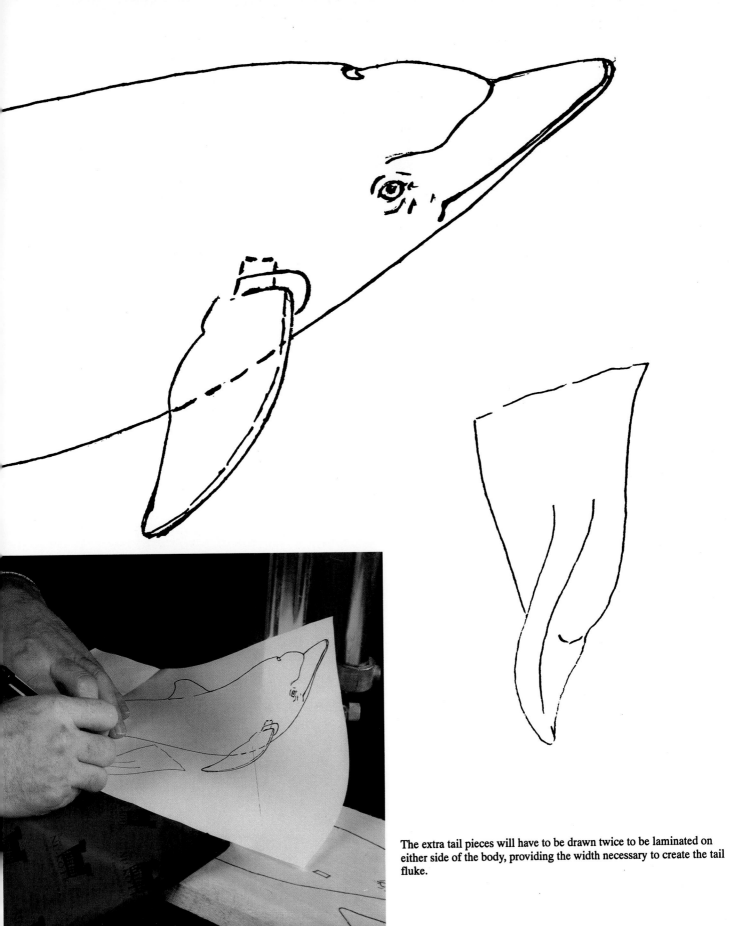

The extra tail pieces will have to be drawn twice to be laminated on either side of the body, providing the width necessary to create the tail fluke.

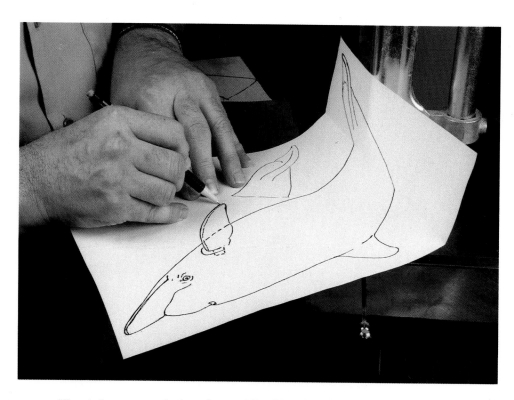

We only have to trace the front fin once. We will cut it in half along its length to make two fins later. Make sure you have traced the fin with the grain running along the length of the fin to lessen the chances of breakage after the carving is finished.

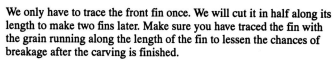

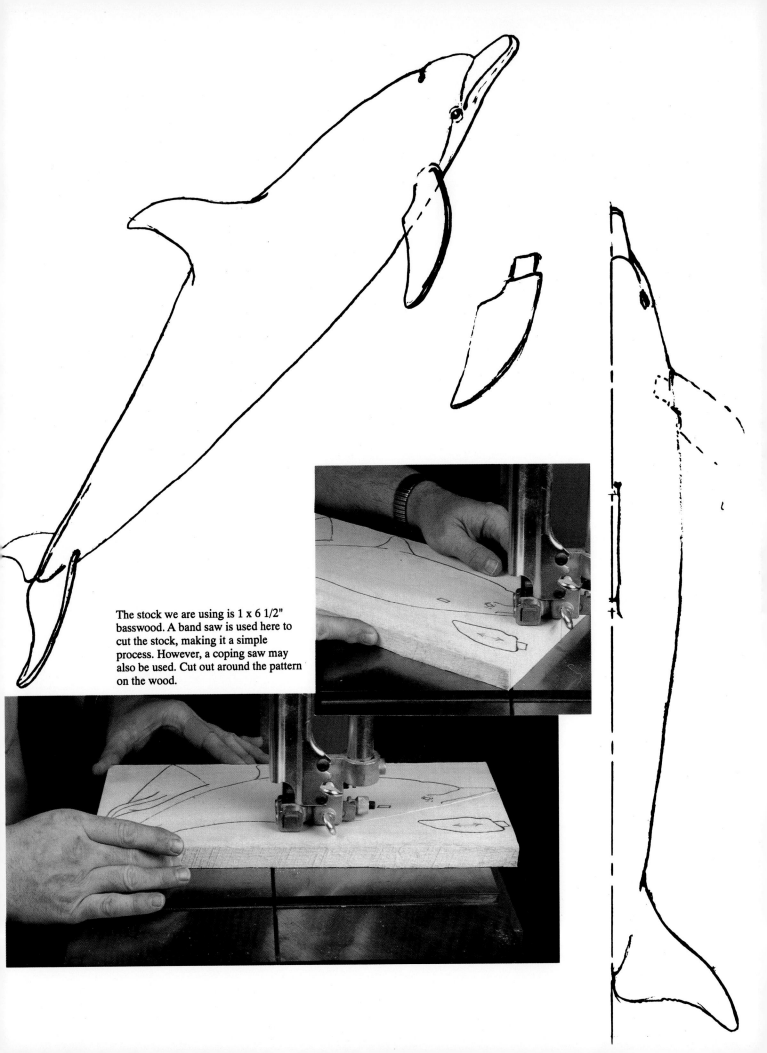

The stock we are using is 1 x 6 1/2" basswood. A band saw is used here to cut the stock, making it a simple process. However, a coping saw may also be used. Cut out around the pattern on the wood.

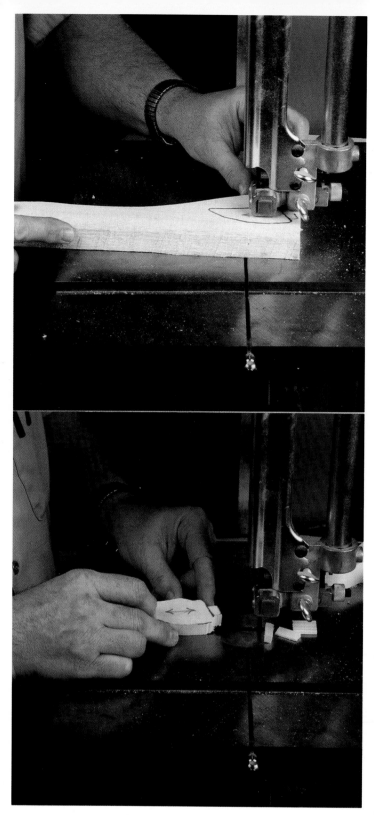

The front fins include a square tenon.

Cut out the fin, following the pattern.

Prior to splitting the fin, mark the centerline all the way around the length of the fin.

Draw in the center line.

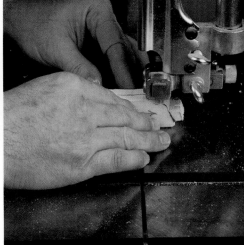

Extreme caution should be used when splitting the fin! Keep your fingers as far from the blade as possible by holding the sides of the wood only and make sure the wood is in good contact with the baseplate before cutting. Once you are sure you are properly prepared, split the fin.

Here are the two fins from the single piece of wood.

All the pieces of the body are laminated together using yellow carpenter's glue. Apply the glue and clamp the body pieces together tightly. There is no such thing as using too many clamps, but if clamps aren't available large rubber bands will hold the piece together securely. Allow the glue to set for twenty-four hours to ensure that the pieces will not separate.

Using the band saw, cut out the tail flukes as well.

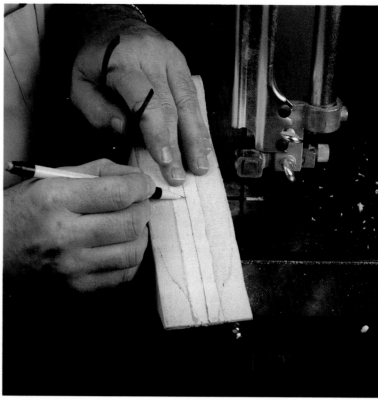

Draw in the center line.

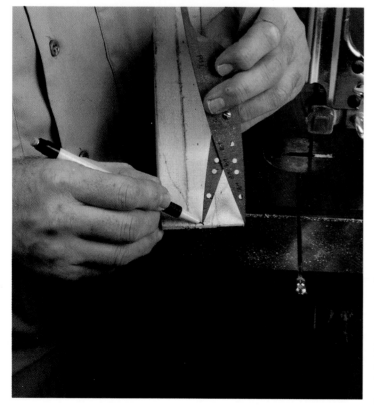

Find the center line along the dorsal view of the dolphin (the top view running along the spine).

Mark the dorsal view of the dolphin, making sure that your carving is torpedo shaped with a smooth flowing line tapering away from the thickest part of the dolphin, from the dorsal fin toward the narrow ends at the nose and the tail.

Keeping your hands well clear of the blade and the wood firmly against the baseplate, cut out the dorsal view of your dolphin.

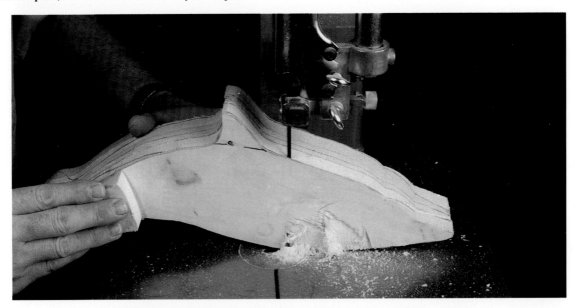

Watch your fingers, you can *not* guarantee the blade will remain in the wood all the way along the side.

Make sure the dorsal fin will fit beneath the blade guide as you cut.

The excess wood is dropping away from the first dorsal view cut.

The second side falls away.

Here is how the dolphin should look now.

We will be rounding the angular edges of the dolphin's body with the band saw. If you do not feel comfortable with this, don't do it (you may hand carve it later). Do not round the tail flukes in any case. Also, do not remove so much stock that you chip off the dorsal fin.

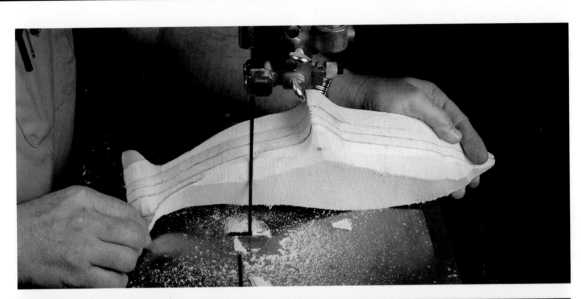

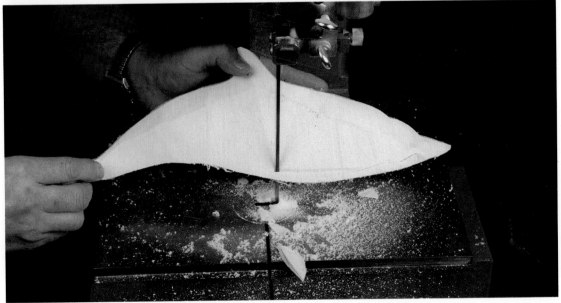

Continue rounding both the top and bottom edges of the dolphin.

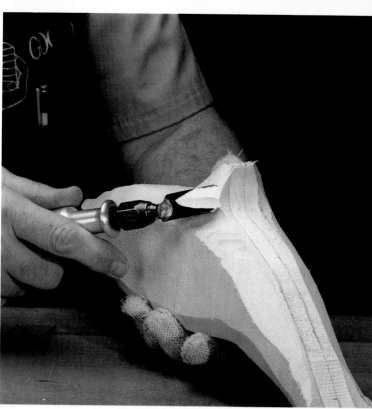

Try to take off the same amount from each side.

Now we will begin the rounding off process using an Automat Powered Wood Carver. This powered chisel speeds up the rounding process. You may use hand-held chisels to do the same job, but the powered chisel makes rounding a little more enjoyable. Begin anywhere you please. I am starting at the dorsal fin. Use the largest chisel you have available to you. I suggest you use a safety glove as it will lessen the chance of injury. The cost of the glove is considerably less than an expensive trip to the emergency room for stitches. These gloves are usually available through any carving supply house.

The rounded dolphin.

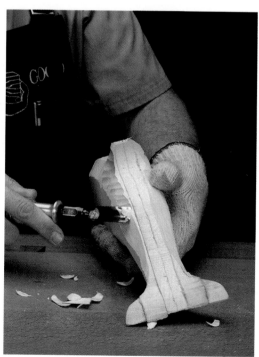

Working along the sharp cut lines left by the band saw, round up to the center line from about half way down the dolphin's side.

Round to the center line in front of the dorsal fin as well. Try not to make your cuts too deep. Any really deep cuts you make will just have to be smoothed out later. Since dolphins are sleek and smooth in form, you don't want to have to reduce them too far to get that shape.

Continue rounding to the center line.

Remove the excess wood from both sides of the dorsal fin, working both sides to keep the carving even.

Draw in a center line along the side of the dolphin. Round the side down to this line.

Round down the dorsal fin.

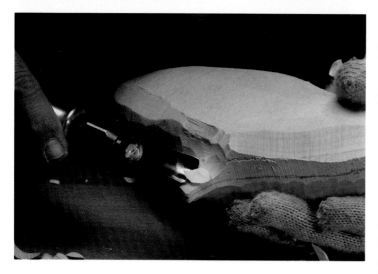

You can't leave the dorsal fin with a large flat area in the back either. You have to round both sides like the hull of a boat, a form which creates no drag in the back. Rounding the back of the dorsal fin.

The valleys in place along the backbone. We will go back and finish them later.

This is how the rounded side should be shaping up. Both sides maintain a uniform shape.

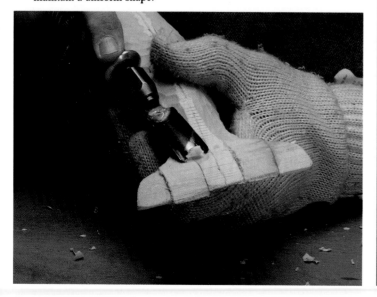

Now I'm forming a little valley on either side of the backbone out onto the fluke.

Here is how the dolphin should look with both sides rounded down. Irregularities will be smoothed down later.

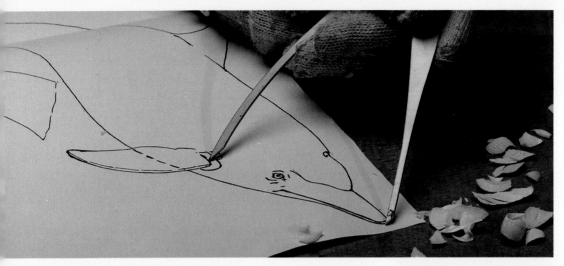

We will move on to the underside of the dolphin. However, before rounding we must determine where the front fins will be placed so we can keep those areas flat. Establish the location of each fin by measuring from the tip of the nose to the front edge of the tenon on the fin.

Transfer the measurement to the drawing with a pencil.

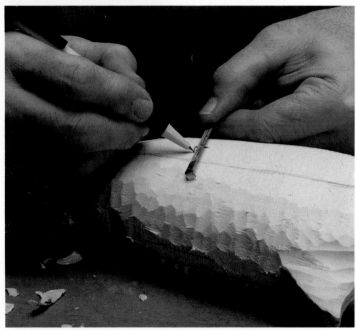

The tenon itself is 3/8" thick. Establish this angle.

From the bottom of the dolphin measure up 3/4" to locate the bottom of the tenon.

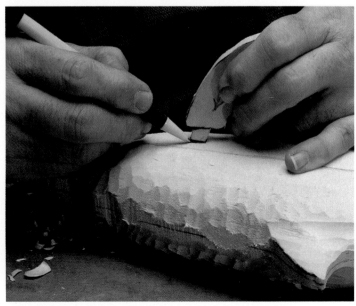

To establish the length of the hole we can use the tenon itself.

17

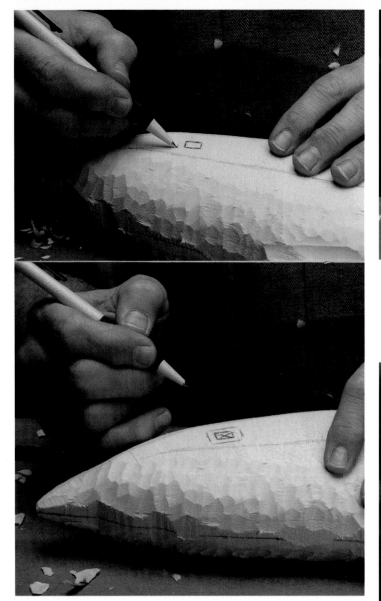

Continue rounding on both sides as you did for the upper body.

Establish the area of the tenon. Leave an area slightly larger than the tenon flat around it. Repeat this process on the other side.

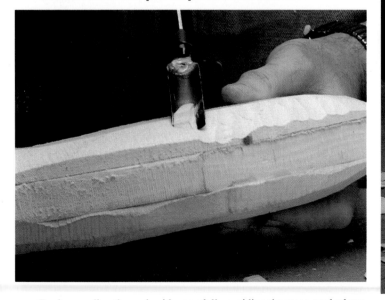

Begin rounding the underside, carefully avoiding the areas marked out for the tenon of the front fins.

The underside should be shaping up like this.

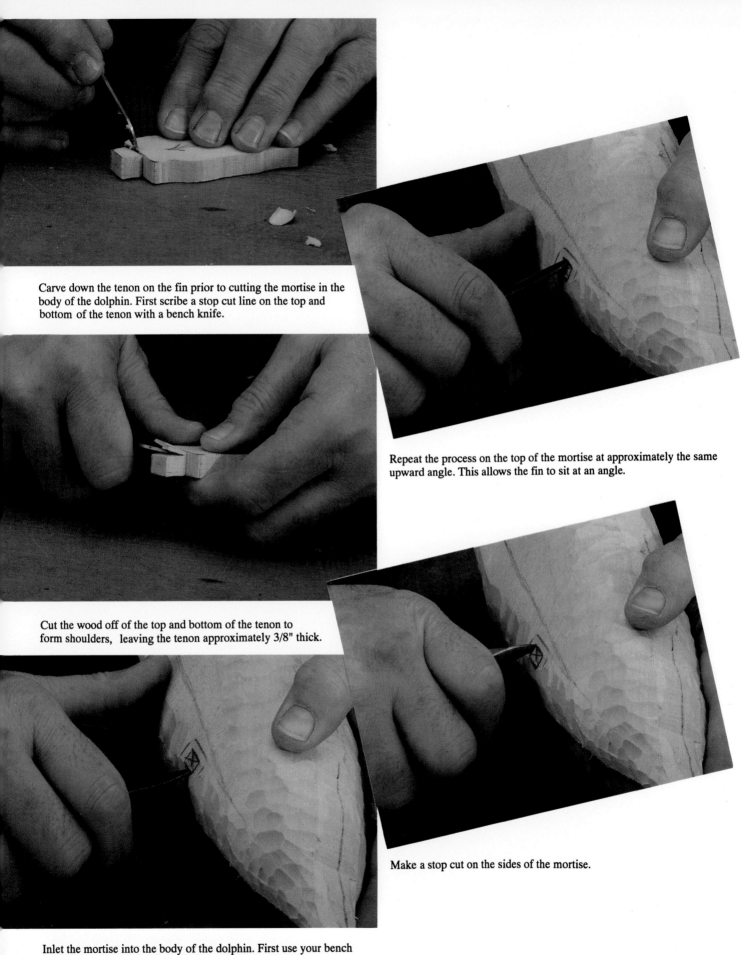

Carve down the tenon on the fin prior to cutting the mortise in the body of the dolphin. First scribe a stop cut line on the top and bottom of the tenon with a bench knife.

Cut the wood off of the top and bottom of the tenon to form shoulders, leaving the tenon approximately 3/8" thick.

Repeat the process on the top of the mortise at approximately the same upward angle. This allows the fin to sit at an angle.

Make a stop cut on the sides of the mortise.

Inlet the mortise into the body of the dolphin. First use your bench knife to cut the base of the mortise at a slight upward slope.

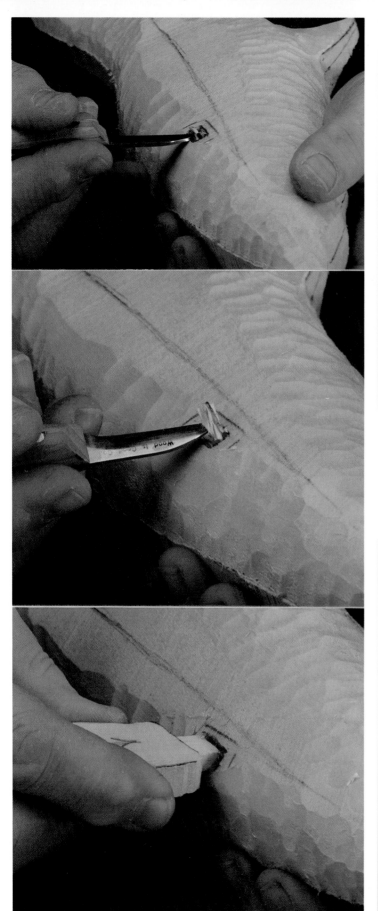

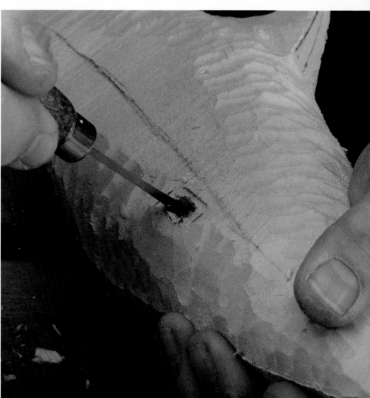

With the chisel, take out small pieces from the mortise.

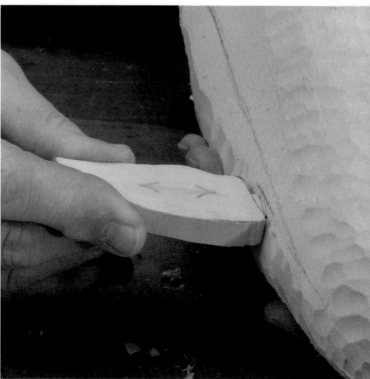

The wood may now be removed either with a bench knife or a small straight chisel. Make a series of cuts across the mortise from front to back, popping thin sections of wood out as you go. Try the fit often.

The fin should slide into place. After making sure the tenon fits into the mortise at the desired angle, set the fin aside. Any desired filling of the joint will be done at the time the fin is glued in place.

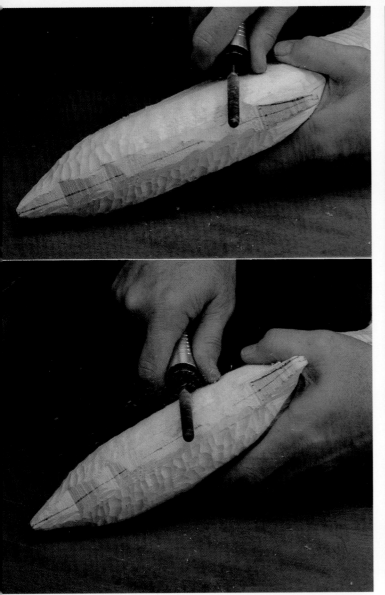

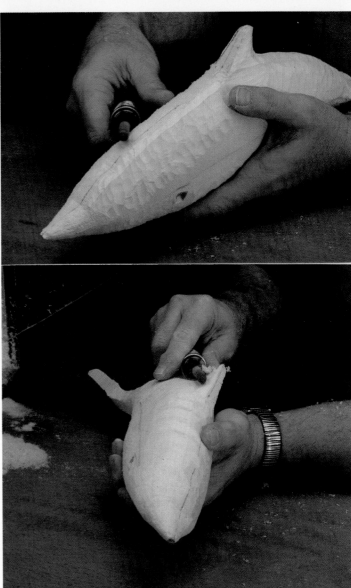

The dolphin with half of the body smoothed.

We are going to switch to a Foredom with a long cylinder Kutzall burr now. Remove the Kevlar glove before switching to the burr. This burr works well when smoothing the large body surfaces of the dolphin. Protect your lungs. Use a dust collection system while working with any rotary tool. Use the Kutzall to begin rounding off the sharp edges along the body.

Continue using the Foredom to smooth out all the deep chisel marks.

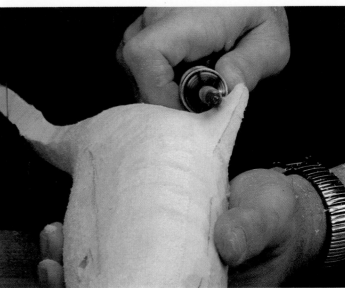

This is the time to shape the dorsal fin, rounding the front and back fin to the center line.

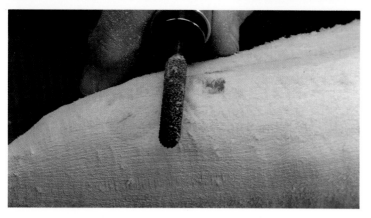

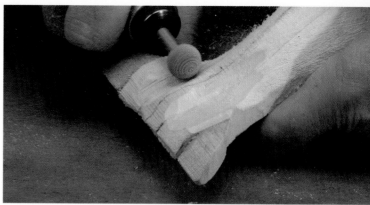

Be careful not to round the area immediately around the mortise as that would make it difficult to get a tight fit when you glue the fins in place.

Use the ball Kutzall to clear out the areas on either side of the spine on the rear fluke.

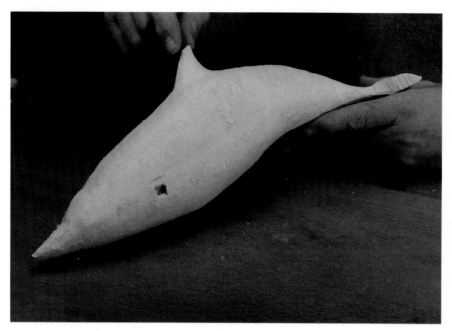

Here is how the rounded body of the dolphin should look at this stage.

Round up this far along the back.

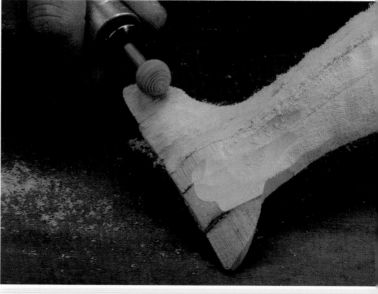

Change the Foredom burr to a 1/2" ball Kutzall.

Form the general shape of the top of the fluke. It is just a slight contour on the top of the fluke. Repeat on both sides.

22

Note the leading edge of the fluke is still shapeless.

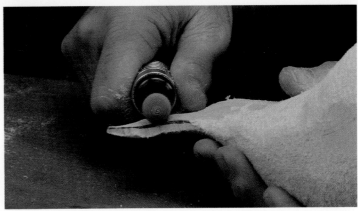

Repeat on both sides of the fluke.

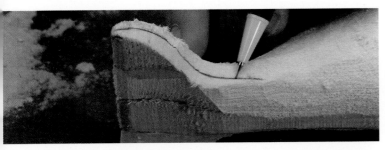

Draw on the line for the leading edge of the fluke. Repeat on both sides. Allow the line to flair out onto the body as you see it here.

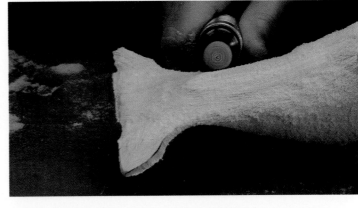

As you shape the fluke, form the section of the body that extends out underneath as a small ridge where muscles attach.

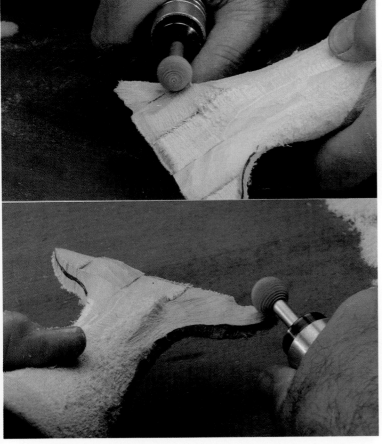

Still using the 1/2" ball Kutzall, begin at the outer tip of the fluke and work your way in toward the center. Work the bottom of the fluke, creating a concave shape.

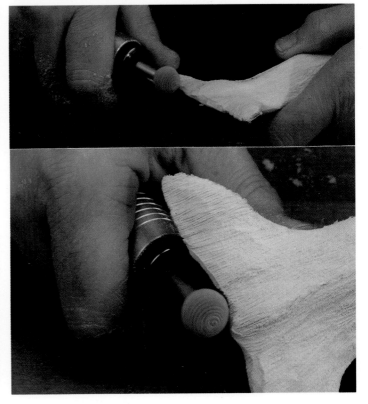

On the upper surface of the fluke, shape the area where the spine ends at the tip of the fluke.

23

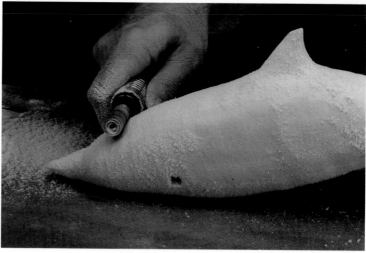

Now it is time to change the Foredom burr to a small 1" x 1/2" sanding device called a Soft Sand. You have to run this at a relatively slow speed to make the 150 grit sand paper last. The slow running speed will keep the sand paper from getting hot and throwing grit too quickly.

Round the head as well.

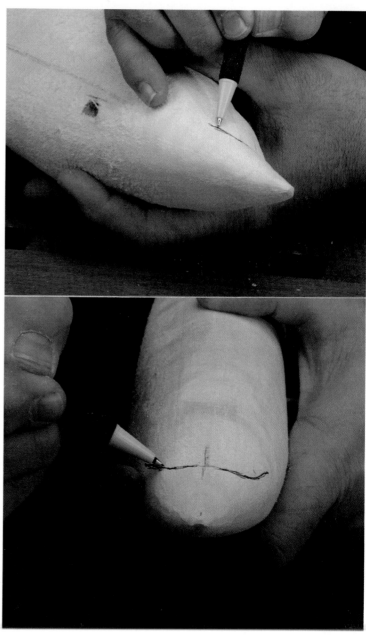

The Soft Sand is used for fine shaping; run it over the entire length of the body. The Soft Sand is also useful for any subtle shaping which needs to be done.

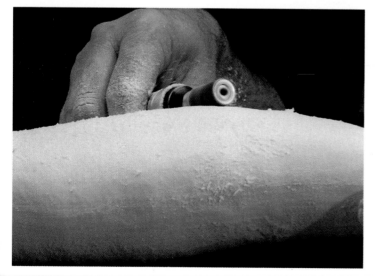

Make sure not to leave a flat area along the side of the dolphin. Shape it into a rounded form with the Soft Sand.

Draw in the groove where the forehead meets the snout.

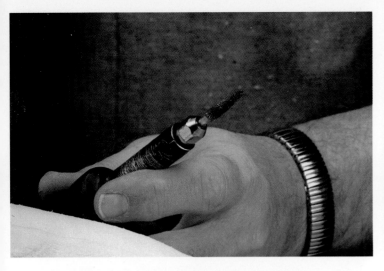

We are going to be using the Optima-2 High Speed Grinder with a small cone shaped Kutzall burr to create this groove.

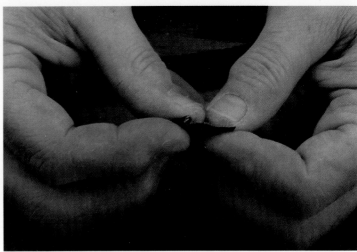

Take a small piece of 150 grit sandpaper, roll it into a tight cylinder ...

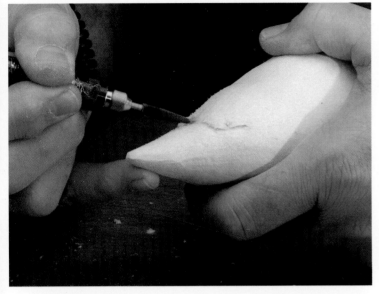

Inscribe the groove where the forehead meets the snout, not too deep and with smooth transition edges. Remember, the dolphin has no sharp lines. The line must be deep enough, however, to remain intact during sanding.

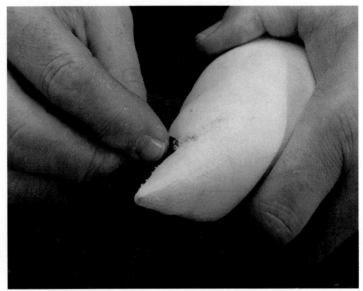

... and use it to finish smoothing the cut you have just made.

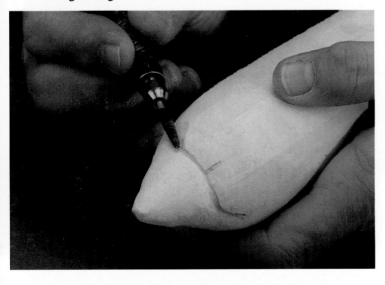

You can see here that the transition line is smooth all around.

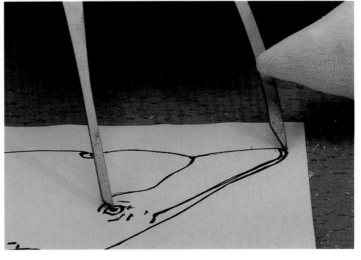

The size of the eye is 3/16" in diameter. Locate the eye by measuring on the plan from the tip of the nose to the center of the eye.

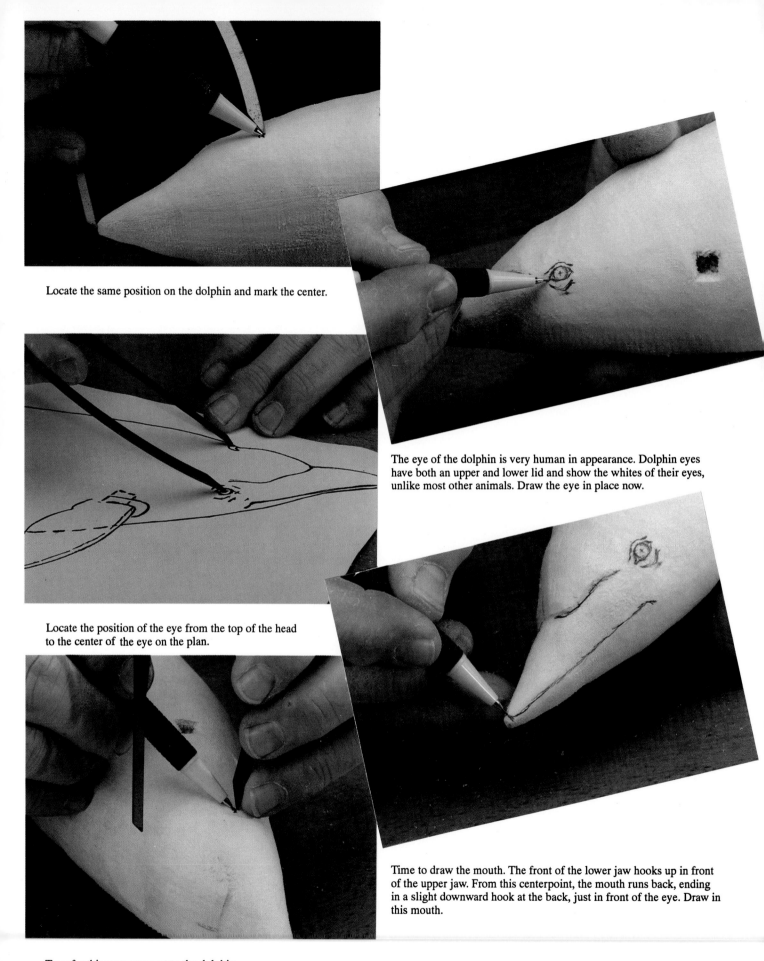

Locate the same position on the dolphin and mark the center.

The eye of the dolphin is very human in appearance. Dolphin eyes have both an upper and lower lid and show the whites of their eyes, unlike most other animals. Draw the eye in place now.

Locate the position of the eye from the top of the head to the center of the eye on the plan.

Time to draw the mouth. The front of the lower jaw hooks up in front of the upper jaw. From this centerpoint, the mouth runs back, ending in a slight downward hook at the back, just in front of the eye. Draw in this mouth.

Transfer this measurement to the dolphin.

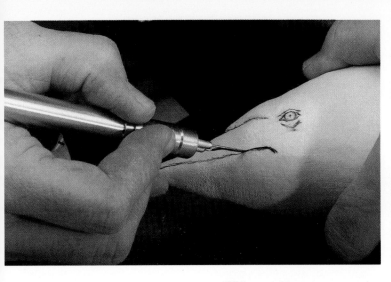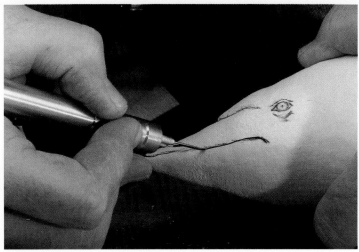

With a wood burner we are going to sculpt in the line of the mouth
and the shape of the eye. Sculpt in the mouth first.

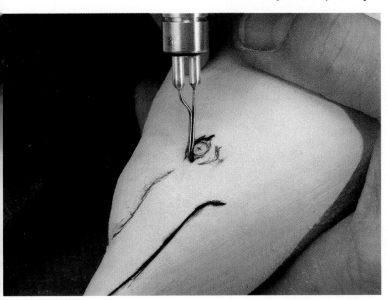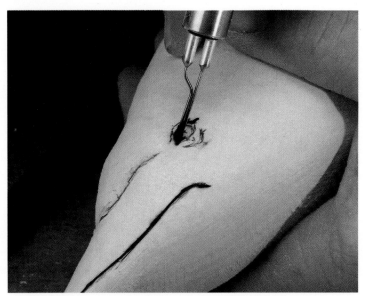

Use the tip as though it is a very fine knife blade. In this way you can
sculpt in the shape of the eyeball itself, along with the lines of the top
and bottom lids.

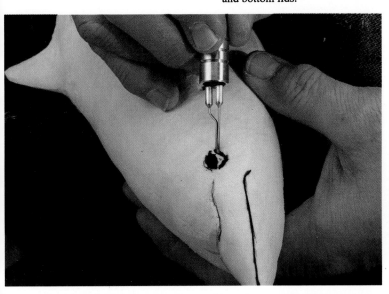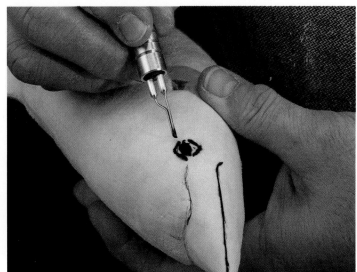

Sculpt in the bottom and top lids of the eye.

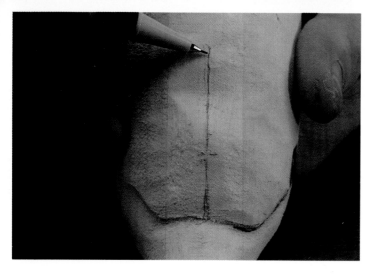

Draw in and sculpt the blow hole at this point. Relocate the center line first.

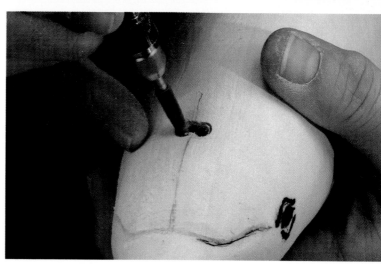

Connect to two holes.

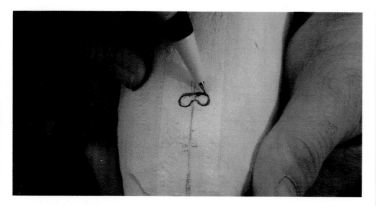

The blow hole, drawn in at the indentation in the head, may vary in appearance but should be slightly kidney shaped.

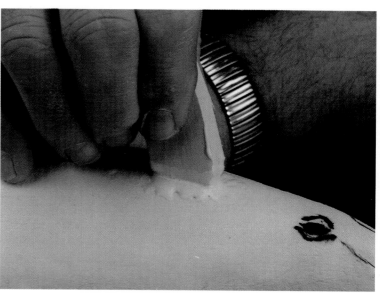

Now fasten the fins by first dipping the tenon of the fin into carpenter's glue and pushing the tenon into the appropriate mortise. Press the fin firmly into place.

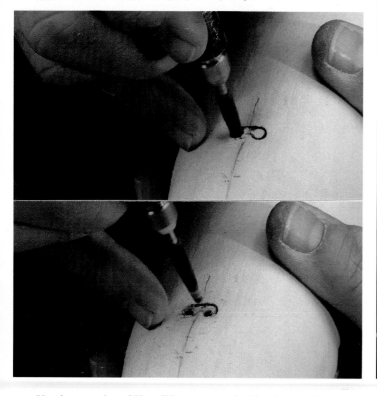

Use the cone shaped Kutzall burr to carve the blow hole, cutting in straight up and down.

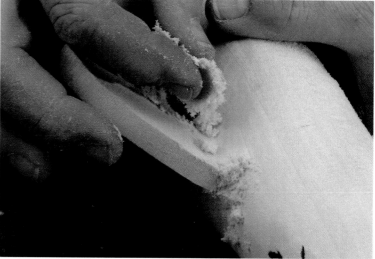

Next pack sawdust into the excess glue that escapes the joint. This acts as excellent filler for any gaps that may be left.

After both fins are in place, set the dolphin aside and let it dry for 12 hours or more until the glue is completely cured.

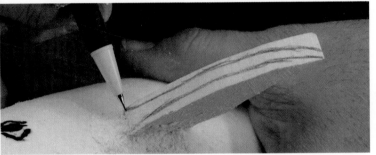

Once the glue has set, draw on the shape of the fins along the leading edge.

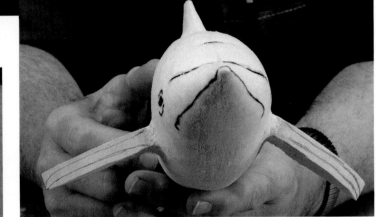

The proper angle of the fin in place.

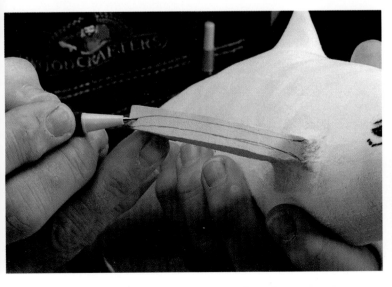

Draw the leading edge in place with a slight downward tilt to the tips. This will give the fins a more life-like appearance.

Indicate a line on the back of the fins showing the shape there as well. The fins are much thinner in the back.

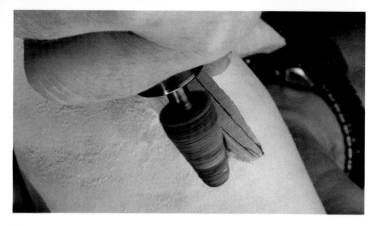

Using a "Christmas tree" shaped Kutzall burr on your Foredom, begin at the tip of the fin. Work inward, shaping the top of the fin first.

Continue shaping down the top of the fin.

To shape the fin into the body it is necessary to flare the fin up onto the dolphin's side. This is accomplished with the Optima-2 high speed grinder fitted with a small "Christmas tree" shaped Kutzall.

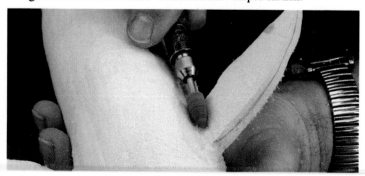

Repeat the process on the bottom of the fin.

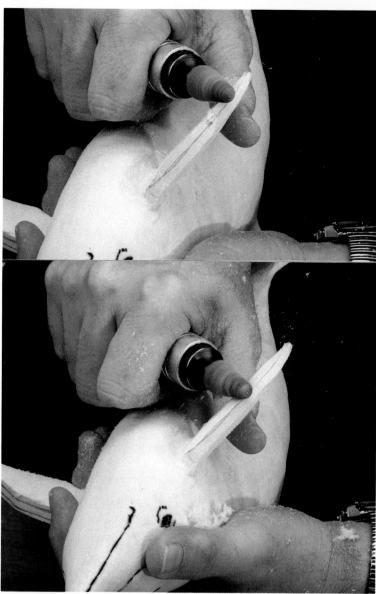

Begin shaping the bottom of the fin with the Kutzall burr, working in from the tip.

The largest amount of material is removed from the back of the fins. The trailing edges are very thin.

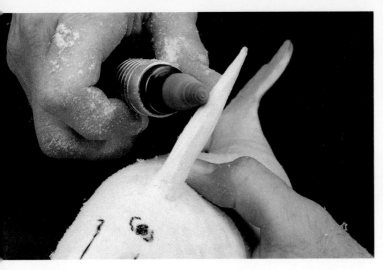

Now round the leading edge on the bottom and the top of the fin. Rounding the bottom.

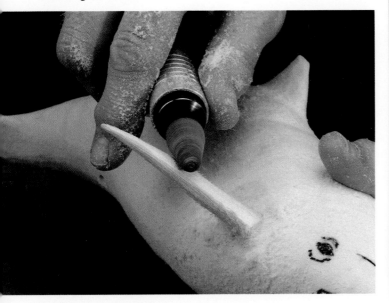

Round the top of the fin.

The shaped fin.

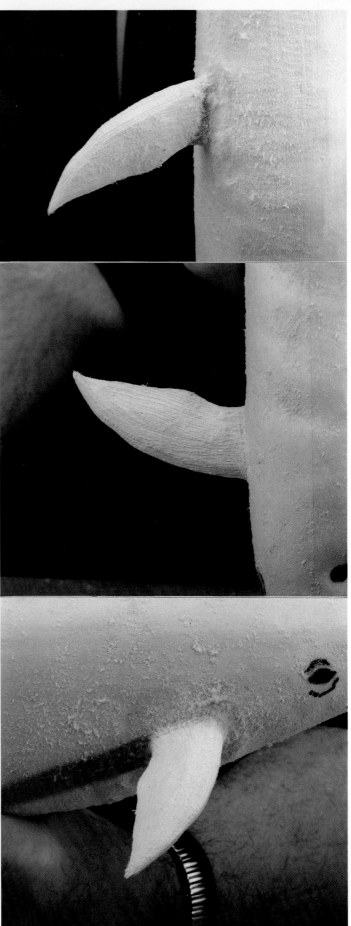

Views of the finished fin.

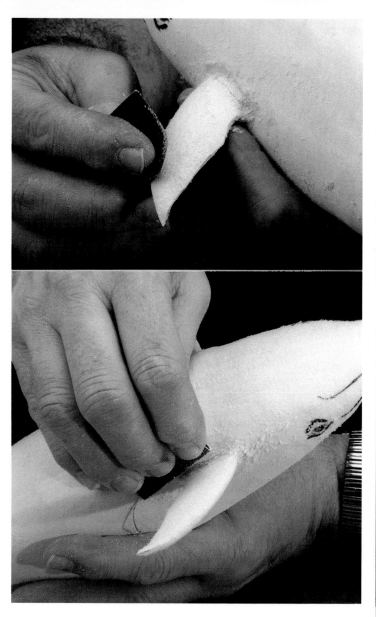

Sand the fins down with 280 grit sandpaper until they are smooth. Any fine blending that needs to be done is done now, smoothing the connection with the body.

Sand carefully around all burned areas to save yourself some work burning in the same areas again.

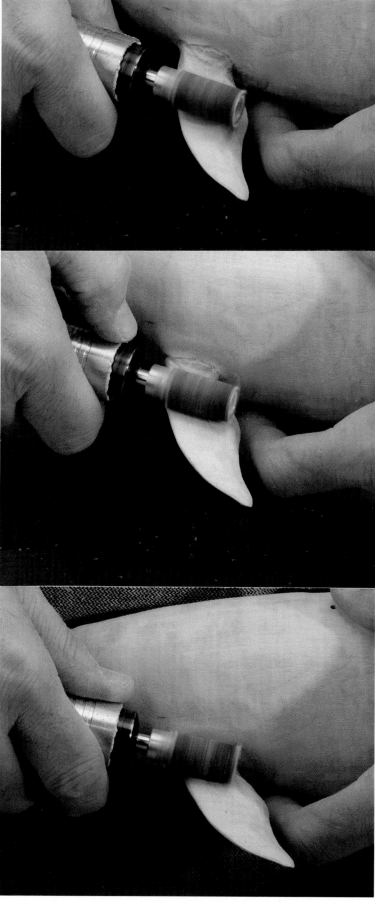

The Soft Sand is used in the final shaping of the fin into the body at this time. Make sure you have a smooth rounded edge on the front of the fin as well.

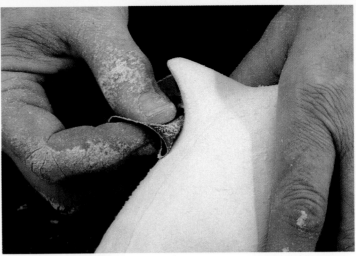

Make sure you sand very carefully behind the dorsal fin to remove any hint of a flattened area.

The fins should look like this.

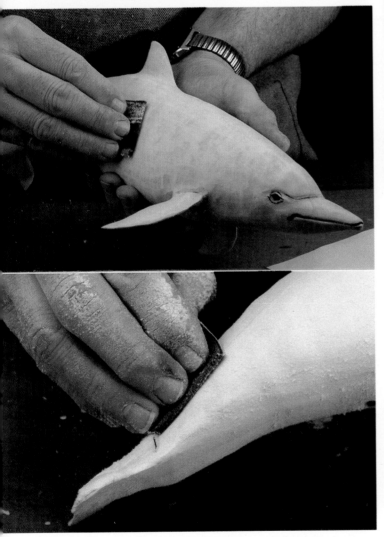

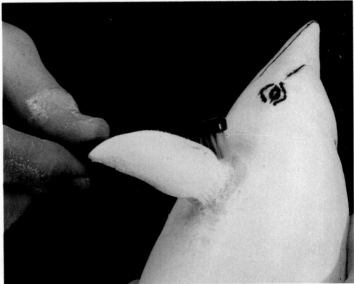

Use a soft bristled toothbrush to remove any wood fibers prior to painting.

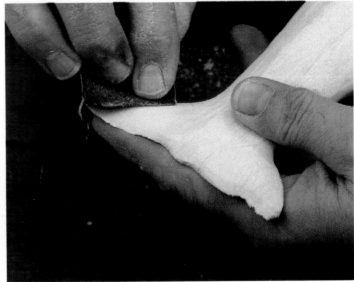

Sand the rest of the body smooth with 280 grit sandpaper.

Support the tail while sanding to prevent breakage.

Sand with the grain and thin the trailing edge. Support the tail very well throughout this process.

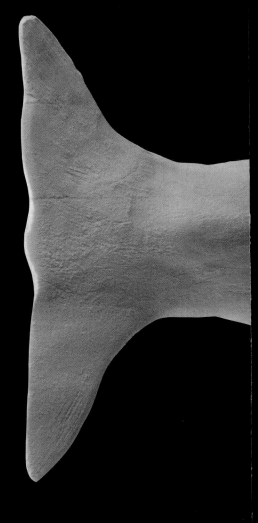

The finished tail fluke.

Make sure the trailing edge of the tail is sanded to a thin uniform edge.

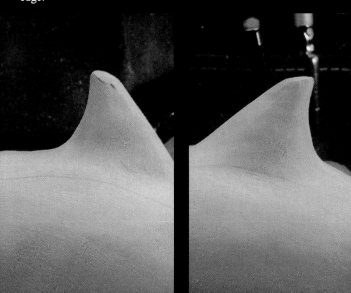

The finished dorsal fin.

The finished dolphin prior to painting.

PAINTING

In the underside of the dolphin, drill a mounting hole at a 45 degree angle.

The gray primer is in place.

Now spray the whole dolphin with a thin coat of clear acrylic. The acrylic spray hardens all the small fibers sticking out of the wood. Once the acrylic has dried, use 250 grit sandpaper to smooth the dolphin, following the grain and removing the fibers. Once sanded, we are ready to paint. The Bottle-nosed Dolphin has a back that is usually dark gray. The sides are a lighter gray shading to pink or white on the belly. A dark cape, almost black or a very deep gray, often extends from the head along the back past the dorsal fin and fades out near the rear flukes. Older females may have a spotted belly. First we will be using a light gray as a primer coat. Add a lot of water to the paint, thinning it way down, and apply it as a light wash.

THE DOLPHIN

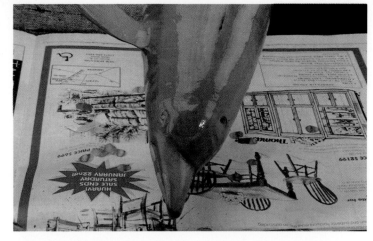

Now mix a little black into the gray to darken it even more. Water it down again to make a wash. Apply this coat starting at the beak (the front of the mouth) and painting up over the back and along the sides down to and out on the top of the fins.

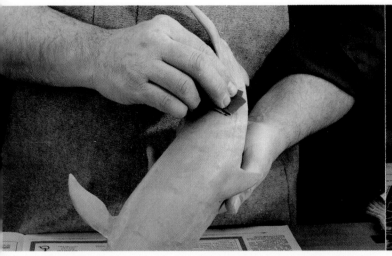

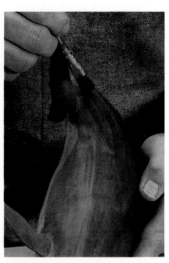

Use 400 grit sandpaper for one more fine sanding, making sure to sand with the grain. This last sanding will remove any small grain fibers that stood up during the application of the gray primer coat.

Take watered down white and paint the underbelly, blending up onto the sides in a very fine thin wash to highlight the gray sides.

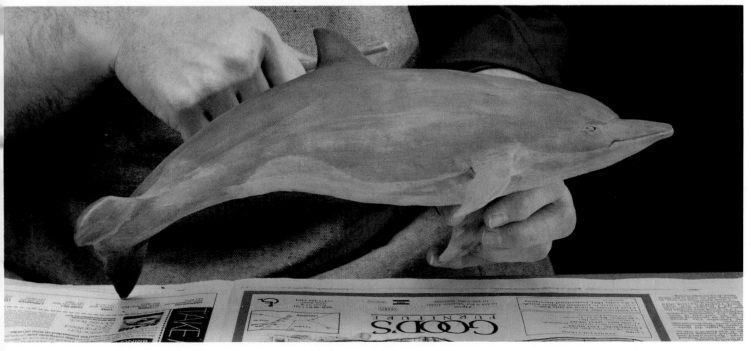

The painted dolphin so far.

Now we are going to apply a final wash of black on the back to form the cape. First we will make definite the black cape, adding a very strong black in the center of the back, up the dorsal fin, and following down the spine--leaving that area the darkest black.

Then take water and start washing the edges to blend them out with the water down onto the sides so that the cape blends into the gray sides.

Load up a small brush with pure black and paint down inside the blow hole.

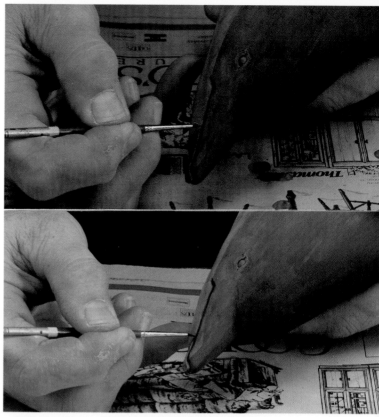

Lay a very fine black line in the cut you made to illustrate the mouth.

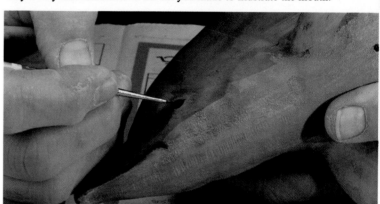

Use black to paint the eyes in on both sides. Use a solid black to begin with.

Dry the painted eyes with a hair dryer to save time.

38

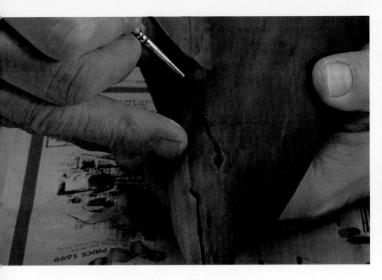

Water down the black paint and add a tear line.

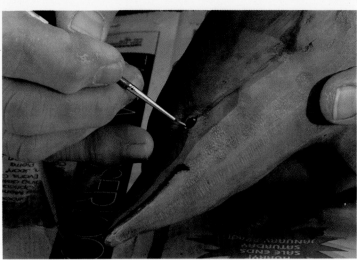

To finish the eyes, water the white paint down a little and, using a very small brush, add just a touch of white in the very front and back part of each eye.

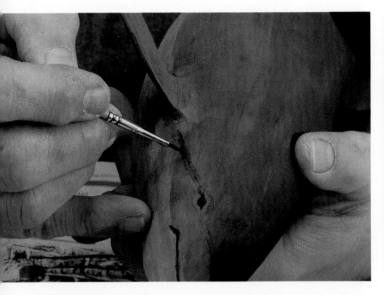

Before it dries, wash out the tear line so that it is just a soft dark stripe.

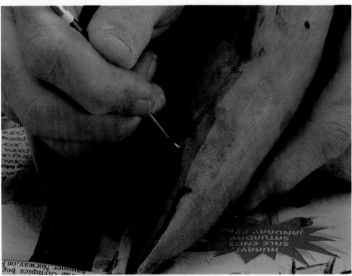

Continuing with the small brush, place two tiny dots of pure white to create the highlights in the eyes.

Add just a touch of very watered down white to highlight the tear line.

As a suggestion, make up a mixture that is 50 percent white Elmer's glue and 50 percent water, paint it on your dolphin with a wide flat nosed brush, and let it dry. This will give you a shiny surface you can either wax over or use a clear acrylic spray over as a finish. Do not worry that it is milky white as you are painting it on. This mix dries clear. However, a word of advice--don't leave too many bubbles.

The finished dolphin.

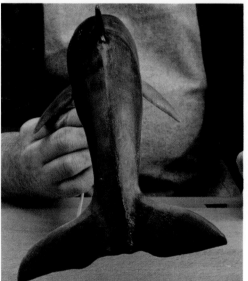

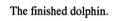

The finished dolphin as part of a larger work featuring three Bottle-nosed Dolphins.

THE STAND

Marbleizing the stand adds a certain eye-catching appeal to your work. Take whatever wood you care to use, sand it to remove any wood fibers and round all the edges prior to painting.

Wipe the surfaces down with 400 steel wool in the direction the grain runs. This removes any abrasiveness.

Now drill a hole at 45 degrees to place the doweling to hold your dolphin.

To make a green marble we're going to mix a bright yellow with a small amount of blue.

Put the sponge directly into the paint.

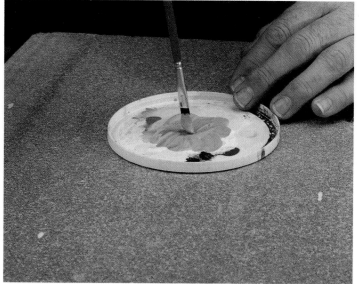

Mix thoroughly so no yellow is showing.

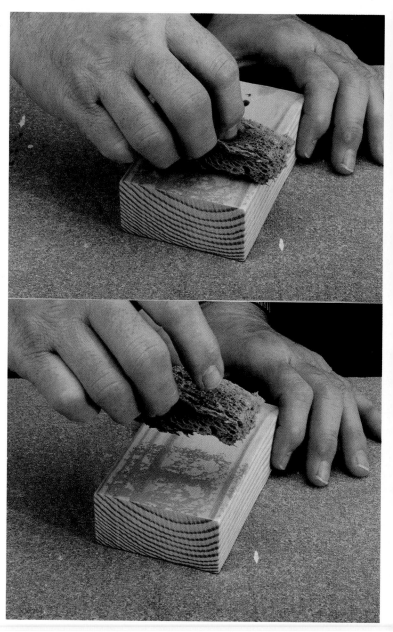

Take a sponge and tear out chunks so there are no square lines. Also tear chunks out of the middle to make an irregular surface.

Place the sponge straight down onto the wood and make sure you pick it straight up. The dowel rod makes a great handle while painting.

Repeat the same action all over the base.

Repeat the painting process in pure black. Use the side of the sponge rolled up this time.

Repeat the process in the opposite direction to make sure the pattern is not regular.

Randomly fill the surface with black patterns. If you run out of paint go back and restart.

Once you have the base coated, set it aside or use a hair dryer to speed the action. The paint must be good and dry before you proceed.

Fill some areas in darker than others.

The black now covers the wood base.

Repeat the sponging with white. The sponge should be rolled up again for this step. Work the white into the sponge a little more than the black because the white is to be a smaller pattern.

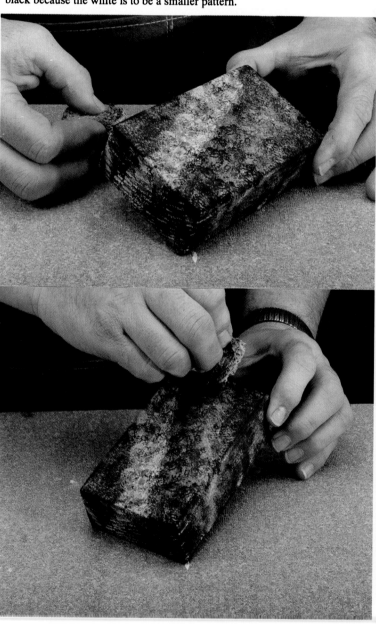

Blacken the dowel as well and dry the paint.

Place in a very random pattern across the piece.

Here's how the base looks so far.

Just let the drifts trail through the piece. They vary from thick to thin. Make sure drifts run all the way down the edge.

Use a small lining brush to apply veins on the faux marble. They are painted in using thinned down black.

Now we will add the drifts (drifts are put in by watering your paint way down). The drifts will run all in one direction. Drifts occur when minerals filter into the forming marble through wide cracks created during shifts in the Earth's crust. Use a number 4 round brush to apply.

Paint the veins in, thinking of them as lightning strikes for the design. They must trail down off the piece.

Keep following along where the white has gone. The veins are produced by minerals which have run down through fine cracks. The more intricate the veining and drifting, the more people seem to like it.

With an even smaller brush, accent the veins with thin white lines.

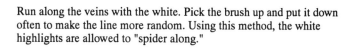

Run along the veins with the white. Pick the brush up and put it down often to make the line more random. Using this method, the white highlights are allowed to "spider along."

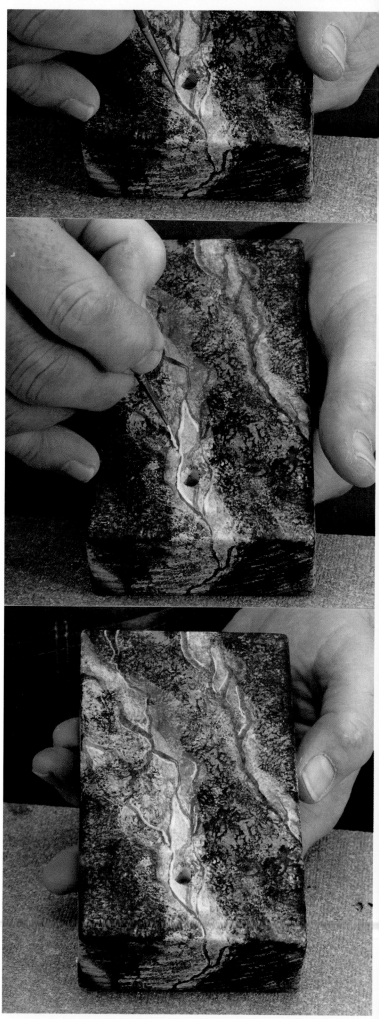

Barely water the black and go back again with the small brush and put in little black highlights like the white ones.

To give the marbleized stand a completely smooth surface, use 400 steel wool and rub in the direction of the grain.

Apply a gloss medium made of 50 percent Elmer's glue and 50 percent water.

Once the gloss medium has dried, take the 400 steel wool and wipe gently in the direction of the grain to smooth any brush strokes out and to polish the surface to give it a marbled look.

More black highlights.

Reapply the gloss mixture perpendicular to the last coat.

We have changed the look of the stand by marbleizing it. We can also change the dolphin's appearance with a little more creative painting. You may prefer your dolphin to appear as if it has been carved from a different material and left with the "natural" wood exposed. To create a faux walnut, we will be using nutmeg brown, black and yellow ocher acrylics. First use a damp sponge to apply nutmeg brown paint over the dolphin as a base coat.

Smooth with the steel wool again. Repeat this process a total of six time...

... and you will have a marbleized base.

Wiping in the direction that the grain flows, cover the entire dolphin.

If glue appears through the paint, go back and add a little more color over that area when it has dried.

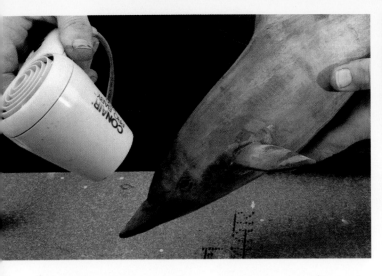

Now that the dolphin is completely covered, here is a quick way to dry him quickly.

Apply a second coat of nutmeg brown with your sponge.

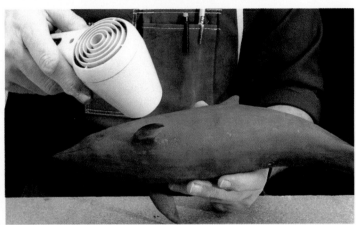

Steal your wife's, husband's or significant other's hair dryer yet again and dry the paint.

Wipe down again with the 400 steel wool.

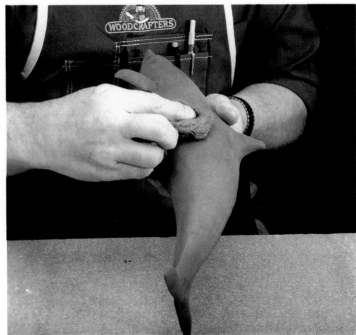

Smooth with 400 steel wool to remove any loose grain that may have been raised after the first coat was applied. The 400 steel wool also does a fine sanding job between each coat of paint. Always wipe in the direction of the grain with a lint free cloth once you have finished sanding.

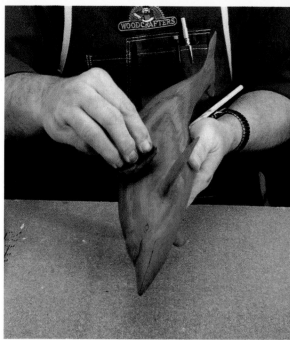

Once you have applied four coats of paint and have wiped each down with steel wool, you are ready to apply the details.

Wipe the dolphin with the steel wool, blending the colors a little as well as smoothing the surface.

Mix yellow ocher and chestnut brown (more yellow ocher than chestnut brown), water it down, and--using a fairly flexible brush--start forming the colors that will delineate the grain of the faux walnut.

Mix a small amount of black into the nutmeg brown and add to create the dark part of the grain that would flow through the walnut. Water your paint slightly to make it flow properly.

The mixture which will highlight the grain is now in place. Dry it completely.

Pull them in together to get a green cast.

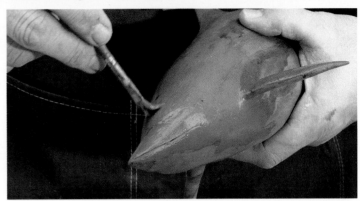

Add the color, approximating the pattern of the previous color application. Since this piece is carved in the round, the colors should encircle the piece.

Paint this mixture on all over but don't let it dry.

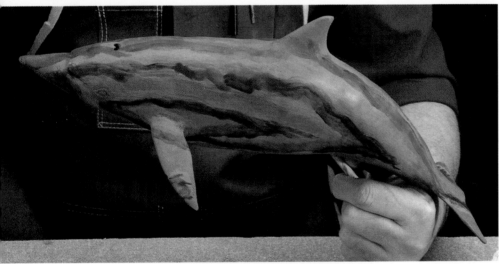

The black and nutmeg brown have been added. Doesn't look like diddley, does it? Wipe it down with steel wool again anyway.

Mix nutmeg brown, a spot of yellow ocher, and a spot of black.

Wipe off the painted area with a course paper towel until the paint underneath starts to show through. The more you wipe, the more your previously painted grain will show through.

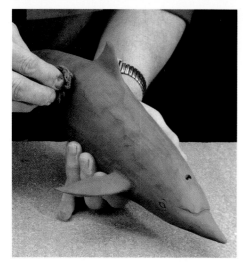
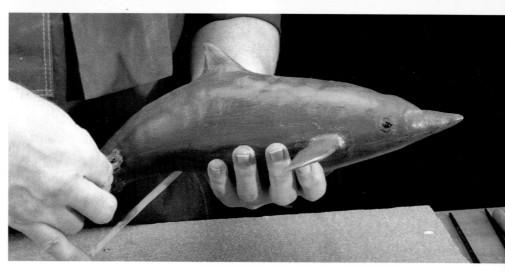

Once the wiping is complete, rub the dolphin along the grain with steel wool. The more you rub with the steel wool, the shinier the paint gets.

Wipe down the dried Elmer's glue mix with 400 steel wool.

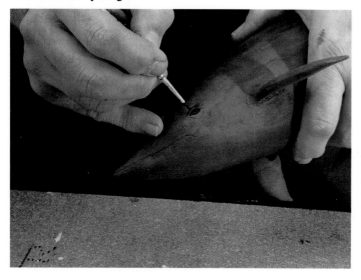
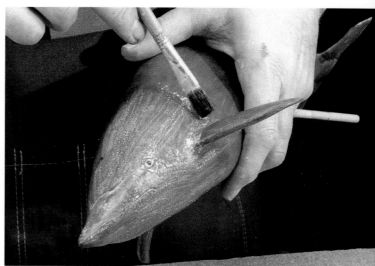

Paint your dolphin's eyes black to make them show up more.

Apply a second coat of the Elmer's mix, a little more watered down this time to hide any brush strokes that may occur. Feel free to experiment until you find what you feel is the right mix.

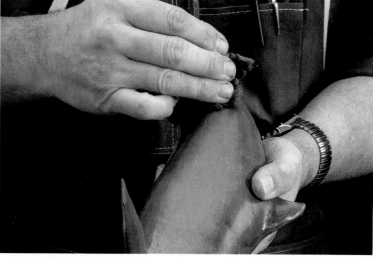

Now add a mixture of 50 percent Elmer's glue and 50 percent water to the dolphin with a brush.

Wipe the dolphin down with steel wool one more time and apply a coat of paste furniture wax to finish the piece.

Now you have a faux walnut dolphin.

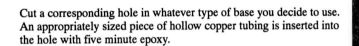

Cut a corresponding hole in whatever type of base you decide to use. An appropriately sized piece of hollow copper tubing is inserted into the hole with five minute epoxy.

To produce the trio of dolphins in the formation you saw earlier, first use five minute epoxy glue to apply a square copper tubing into the back of the bottom dolphins.

Two holes are drilled in corresponding spots where the middle dolphin will fit. They are 3/16" holes.

The lower dolphin is now in place.

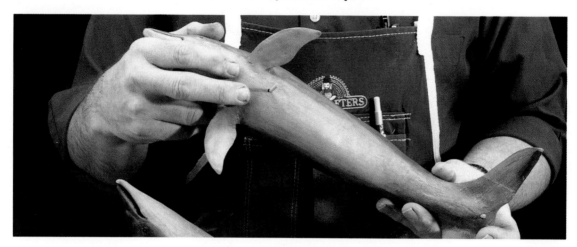

On the middle dolphin, insert 1/8" doweling into the holes and glue into position with five minute epoxy.

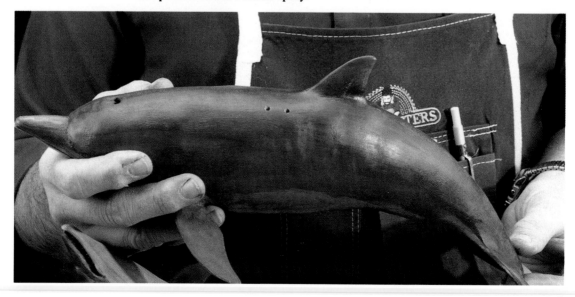

Drill two more 3/16" holes in the top of the middle dolphin, spaced approximately 1/2" apart.

Insert doweling into the holes in the lower dolphin and glue the middle dolphin in place with five minute epoxy.

Drill two 3/16" holes 1/2" apart in the belly of the little dolphin on top to match the holes in the middle dolphin. Insert 1/8" doweling and glue into place with five minute epoxy.

Insert doweling into the holes in the top of the second dolphin with five minute epoxy and glue the little dolphin in place.

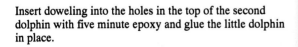

THE GALLERY

56

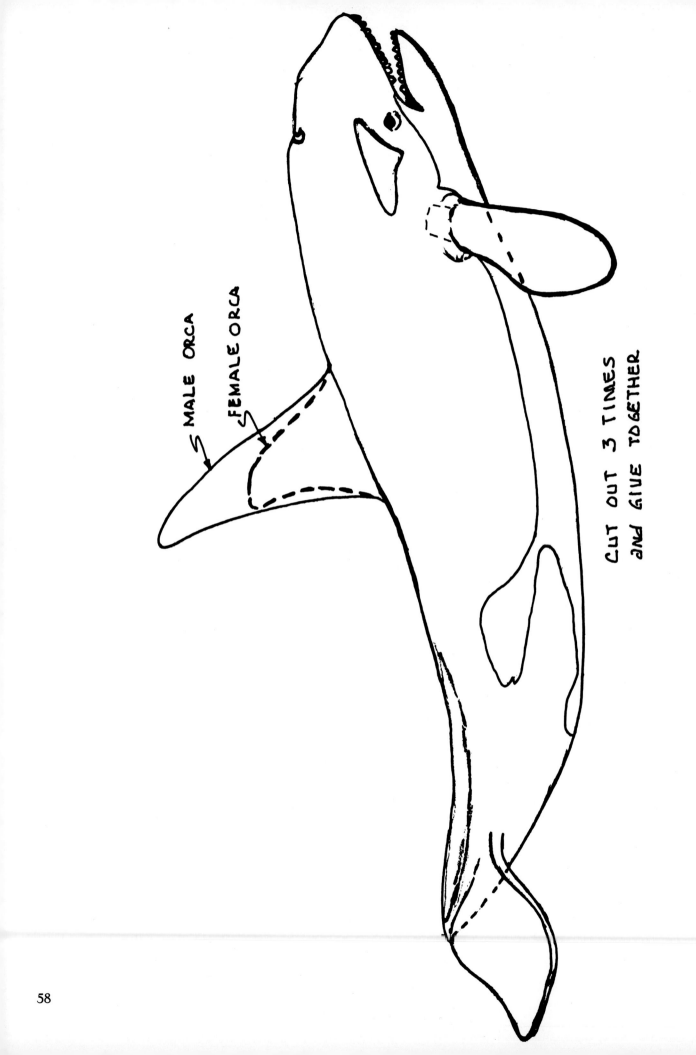

MALE ORCA

FEMALE ORCA

CUT OUT 3 TIMES AND GLUE TOGETHER

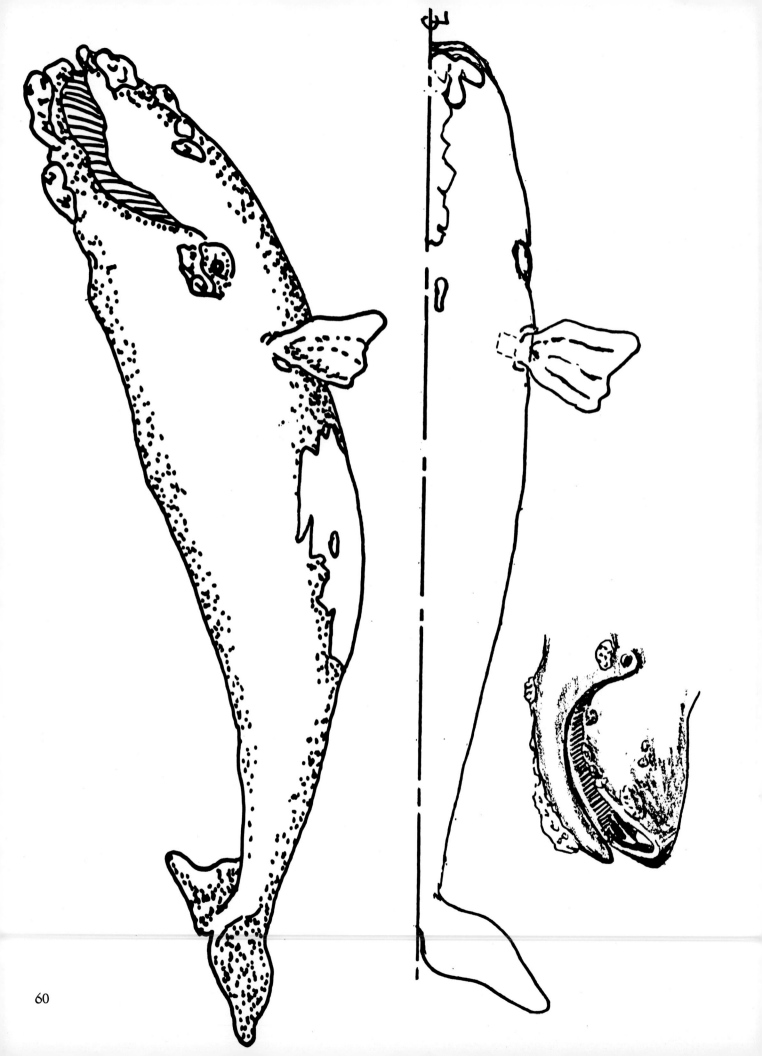